WRITERS REPUBLIC

REFLECTIONS

MICHAEL FISHER

This publication contains the opinions and ideas of its author. It is intended to provide helpful and informative material on the subjects addressed in the publication. The author and publisher specifically disclaim all responsibility for any liability, loss, or risk, personal or otherwise, which is incurred as a consequence, directly or indirectly, of the use and application of any of the contents of this book.

WRITERS REPUBLIC L.L.C.
515 Summit Ave. Unit R1
Union City, NJ 07087, USA

Website: *www.writersrepublic.com*
Hotline: *1-877-656-6838*
Email: *info@writersrepublic.com*

Ordering Information:
Quantity sales. Special discounts are available on quantity purchases by corporations, associations, and others. For details, contact the publisher at the address above.

Library of Congress Control Number: 2021913411
ISBN-13:   978-1-63728-664-7   [Paperback Edition]
                  978-1-63728-665-4   [Digital Edition]

Rev. date: 06/24/2021

Reflection

You had me going

Emotions were flowing

At least those were mine

You had me dreaming

Soon to believing

That you were with another guy

Every time I look into your eyes

I see a reflection and it's not mine

Whenever I look at you

I see love that's glowing but it's not from me and you

You had me thinking

Marriage is the reason

But that reason became untrue

My love was growing

Soon to be knowing

That my heart will become shattered and broken

But if I only knew

Every time I look into your eyes

I see a reflection and it's not mine

When he looks into your eyes

What does he see?

Does he see a reflection of me?

Promise Me

I don't want to be your past

I want a future…with you

I'm trusting you with the key to my heart

Promise me, you won't rip it apart

I refuse to be your rebound that expected…love

But was neglected

Because of your past tense wanting a future

I've given up on love before

But I will give this a try for the last time

After this, I'm done

I don't want you to become my past

But I want a future…with you

I Miss You

We were closer than photos in an album

Deeper than the ocean

Unspoken words left us undefined

What happened to us?

Never wanted to leave each other's side

Like Twin Pops we were always together

Heated disagreements drifted us apart

What was that for?

I blame you

But instead, I will take the fall

Going from I love you

To rejecting phone calls

Going from moments sweeter than a Hershey's kiss

To moments that I must forget

You were the only one I could share my secrets with

Now you're gone

I'm living life with full of regrets

Wish I could rewind what happened

Became a mature adult

And not let you get in the car

Instead of yelling I hope you never come back

Apologized for my childish acts

Looking at my phone to see if you will call or text

Being in this house, will never be the same

Now that you're gone…I miss you

I Rather Be Alone

No more arguments

No more making up

No more happiness or sadness

No more being in love

No more falling out

No more starting over

Or trying to get to know each other

I rather be alone

I'm tired of going through the same cycle with different people

I don't want to fall in love with the wrong person

I know we are not perfect

But I'm perfect for me

No worries about my significant other

Wondering if you're going to find another lover

I will forever be happy, strong, independent, and most of all free

That's why I would rather be with nobody but me

A Piece of Me

In my room…sitting…

Thinking about what just happened

I was a fool to let you see a side of me

Now that you're gone, you took a piece of me

Why did I open my heart?

Why did I tell you all my secrets?

Promising you would never tell a soul

If I could rewind and take that all away

Maybe I would be happy today

If I could erase that night

Then maybe I could sleep better tonight

All you wanted was one thing

And now you want me to forget it

You say it was so unexpected

But I say I regret it

All you wanted was a piece of me and I was dumb to give in

I wish I were done with you, like you're done with me

But I just can't get over the way you mistreated me

I'm sitting in my room...thinking...

I was a fool to let you see a side of me

Now that you're gone you took a piece of me

Broken Promises

You're full of broken promises

Misleading actions

How did this happen?

To someone that I thought I could trust

Love mistaken for lust

But I must get over the fact you lie

Every single time

How could I be so blind

Real love is so hard to find

Stupid of me to think it exist

I think I'm over all of this

Friends, family, and even myself

I don't need nothing from nobody else

Because you're full of broken promises

Misleading actions

Why did this happen to me?

I trusted the wrong people and the only
person I can blame is me

We Can Make It

We have our ups

We have our downs

But we will always have each other around

We may agree

We may disagree

I don't care as long as you're here with me

Whatever God has in store for us

I'm ready for the challenge

Only if you're down for the ride

Promise me you will stay by my side

Through the good days and bad

Happy or sad

For rough and for worse

Promise me you won't leave

Our past hasn't been the greatest

But trust me

We can make it

He Better Be

I hope he gives you everything you deserve

I hope he makes you smile

I hope he makes your heart sing

Cause since you left me

He better be your everything

I hope he gives you cards and flowers

Takes you to the movies and a dinner after

Buys you a nice car and fancy clothes

Treats you better than all the ones before

He better be God's best creation

Your Prince Charming

Living a fairy tale

Better than us

He better be your everything

I wish you the best

Since you decided to move on to the next

To think I was going to pop the question

Thinking I was your absolute blessing

Tell me,

Is he worth leaving me?

Give me a reason…a reason why

Don't walk away, sit here and watch me cry

Is he worth sacrificing everything you love?

He better be

Do Better Blues

How fast will it take for this to crash?

How tight will it take for this to crumble?

How big of a crack to make us trip and fall?

How many times do I have to reject your phone call?

How many pain pills will it take to get over you?

How many times I have to look in the
mirror and say I'm over you

Will these tears on my pillow make the pain go away?

I have to do better and get over you…today

How long do I have to drive?

Run away from civilization and hide

How about we skip the cries

No emotion

Just a simple

Goodbye

Just go on about our day

Take our phones out and throw the battery away

Burn pictures and depart ways

How long does it take to let go of the one you love?

How many years does it take?

I must do better and get over you… today

Palm Roll Twist

When we expressed our love

We meant it

Advised ourselves to take things slow

Cleaned ourselves from our past

As we grow

You grab what is new

I do a little twist to show that I love you

Then I place your heart in my hand to show that I care

And roll our memories into my hair

Place the clip so these memories can properly lock

My love is growing and will never stop

Brand New

I'm turning into a new leaf

Removing all sorrow and grief

Leave the past in the past

And just remember good things which would last

Forgive those who will not forgive you

For it is the best thing you should do

Leaving all my stress

And stop getting angry

For this is a new year for me

Or a new day to be. Free

If Love Were Young

If all the world and love were young

It would rise like the morning sun

Then it will fall like a sunset so quick

As we began to think this love is sick

Because love can be so good, you just get tired of it

As were young we fall in love fast

And we fall out so quick that our moments never last

I will take this chance to be your man

Ride this love roller coaster as long as I can

I'm ready for the ups and downs

The twist and turns

And when we crash it will be a lesson learned

That we weren't meant to be

If love were young

Like you and me

It may not last, but I will take this chance

This chance to be your man

Save Me

Save me from my past

Save me from the spell that the devil cast

Bring peace into my life

Take away all misery and strife

Watch over me as I sleep at night

Take me out the darkness so I can see the light

I want to feel your love as it shines so bright

Please save me from my past

Save me from the spell that the devil cast on me

Holding You Close

Every time I hold you

I close my eyes

I never want to let go

I don't know why

Your scent smells so good to me

Every time I'm holding you close

Every time I look into your eyes

I see an angel

Every time I speak to you

My words get twisted or tangled

Holding you is like a dream come true

But what I'm really saying is I love you

I'm Still In Love

I've never felt this way before

It's like a piece of me left when you walked out the door

I know we are not together anymore

No one can take your place and just restore

We weren't ready for commitment

Just drama over again and again

But now I know I lost what was a part of me

I think I'm…Still…In…

But it's hard for me to say

I dream about you almost every day

So why is it hard to say L-O-V-E

When it just you and me

Maybe cause it's my first time

If only I can go back in rewind

And say…i'm…in…

I can't say it to you

I guess I don't love you…but I do

Although it may be late for me to go back

All I want to say it that

Okay, just relax

All I want to say is…

I'm…Still…In…in…

I Am

I am someone

Just like you

I have flaws

But you do too

So don't bring me down

Because I'm not like you

I am

Beautiful

I am

The angel that God made

I am

A human that walks on this earth

I am

The soul within that can't be hurt

I am

Someone just like you

I may have flaws but you do too

I am

Beautiful

Inside and out

I am

Someone who cares about

My life

I am

Have You Ever

Have you ever loved someone that it makes your heart sing?

Have you ever loved someone that

You will give up anything to keep them happy inside

And forget what people say besides

They have never been in love like me and you

I'll give up everything just to be with you

Have you ever?

Talked on the phone and can't get off

And once when you do you feel like you
lost something a part of you

And you want to call back and say

I love you so much that I don't want to get off the phone

I miss your voice, your touch

I just don't want to be alone

Have you ever?

Held your pillow so tight

Wishing that they were there so you can sleep well at night

Have you ever?

Prayed for them more than yourself

Praying to God saying

I'd rather die than see them with someone else

Have you ever loved someone?

You can't find the words to say

How much I love you and how I will always stay

Through Walls

I'm walking through the pain

Looking for what it will gain

I'm bringing happiness back into my life

By walking through the darkness into the light

Each breakthrough reminds me of my grief

I'm happy that this happened to me

As God as my witness

And my provider

He's my GPS system

He's a guider

To help me though these walls

To find my right place

To take this run and win this race

I will reach my goals

And I will hold my head high

As I walk through these walls

Praising his name so high

Silent

I love you…

I…I love you…

I SAID I LOVE YOU!!!

Her voice continues to rise

As the clouds began to cover the skies

The whispering wind starts to become filled with rage

Thunder roars with so much hate

But I continue to stay…

Silent

I Wish I Never Fell In Love

I used to hang on to your every word

I mean your every word

Even the lies

Saying you changed

Telling me you're at work

But you're in the streets doing what only God knows

What would you do if you were in my shoes?

I love you and I know things won't change

Because you're doing the same things

Why do I keep coming back?

I just want my heart back

I wish I never fell in love

Fall

I tried to call

You wouldn't answer my calls

I'm starting to think this relationship will fall

I love you so much to let this relationship dissipate

When we are together, nothing matters I can't concentrate

But when I try to speak

Your answers get weak

I try to be a good man and call

You're out with your friends

Is this relationship falling?

Or do you want me to be a man and stop stalling

Fall in Love

I fell in love

Right into your cosmic sky

Looking into the brightness of those eyes

Those eyes are the key to your inner beauty

The softness of your skin

I just give in and

Fell in love

I fell in love so deeply

That it's sexy when you're mad

Cute when you're sad

But keeping you happy is the prize

That smile and the way your face glows

Keeps me lifted

Your gifted by the way you do your day-
to-day routines without stress

I'm inspired

Over a billion people on this earth

And you chose to be with me

I will do anything to keep you in love with me

Goodbye, Tina

We have so many good memories

Late nights, staying up laughing about life

Enjoying each other's company

But it's time for me to say goodbye

Never thought this day would come

And it has

I must cut you lose and say goodbye

All the places you've shown me

Only you have gotten to really know me

I just can't let you go but I have to

It's a shock to me as it is to you

That's why I'm saying goodbye and leaving

Thinking of You

You've been on my mind for some time now

Wondering what you're doing and who's wasting your time

I see you're still texting me

But I don't reply now

I used to laugh at the jokes you spit

Now I sit here thinking about the good times

I miss them

I find myself replying to your messages

Hey…what are you doing…okay…
can we hang out one last time?

It never gets that far

But what if I do

I don't know why but sometimes when I'm alone

I tend to think of you

A Broken Heart

It was just one

Now its shattered and gone

As the wind blow the pieces away

Like pieces of paper on a windy day

I gather some of the pieces

The ones that I could see

I put them back together and saw a reflection of me

Tears on me face as I'm putting the pieces back into their part

Trying to forget the one who broke my heart